The
Realistic
Joneses

The
Realistic
Joneses

WILL ENO

THEATRE COMMUNICATIONS GROUP
NEW YORK
2015

The publication of *The Realistic Joneses* by Will Eno, through TCG's Book Program, is made possible in part by the New York State Council on the Arts with the support of Governor Andrew Cuomo and the New York State Legislature.

TCG books are exclusively distributed to the book trade by Consortium Book Sales and Distribution.

LIBRARY OF CONGRESS CATALOGING-IN-PUBLICATION DATA

Eno, Will, 1965–
The realistic Joneses / Will Eno.—First edition.
pages ; cm
ISBN 978-1-55936-474-4 (paperback)
ISBN 978-1-55936-792-9 (ebook)
1. Neighbors—Drama. 2. Married people—Drama. 3. Interpersonal relations—Drama. I. Title.
PS3555.N652R43   2015
812'.54—dc23   2015010009

Book design and composition by Lisa Govan
Cover design by Mark Melnick
Cover photograph by Getty Images

First Edition, May 2015

To Tracy Letts

Acknowledgments

With thanks to: Mark Barton, William Berlind, Amy Boratko, Maggie Brohn, James Bundy, Ty Burrell, Toni Collette, Michael Crea, Johanna Day, Glenn Fitzgerald, Susan Gallin, Sam Gold, Michael C. Hall, Jennifer Kiger, Tracy Letts, Stacey Mindich, Victoria Nolan, Christopher Pineda, Parker Posey, Jeffrey Richards, Mary Lu Roffe, Andy Sandberg, Anne Seiwerath, Catherine Sheehy, Mark Subias, Daniel Swee, Marisa Tomei, Steve Traxler, Will Trice, Rachel Viola and David Zinn.

The
Realistic
Joneses

PRODUCTION HISTORY

The Realistic Joneses received its world premiere on April 20, 2012 at Yale Repertory Theatre (James Bundy, Artistic Director; Victoria Nolan, Managing Director) in New Haven, Connecticut. It was directed by Sam Gold; the set design and costume design were by David Zinn, the lighting design was by Mark Barton, the sound design was by Ken Goodwin; the production stage manager was Jenna Woods. The cast was:

BOB JONES	Tracy Letts
JENNIFER JONES	Johanna Day
JOHN JONES	Glenn Fitzgerald
PONY JONES	Parker Posey

The Realistic Joneses opened on Broadway on April 6, 2014 at the Lyceum Theatre. It was directed by Sam Gold; the set design was by David Zinn, the costume design was by Kaye Voyce, the lighting design was by Mark Barton, the sound design was by Leon Rothenberg; the production stage manager was Jill Cordle. The cast was:

BOB JONES	Tracy Letts
JENNIFER JONES	Toni Collette
JOHN JONES	Michael C. Hall
PONY JONES	Marisa Tomei

Characters

BOB JONES, male, 40s
JENNIFER JONES, female, 40s

JOHN JONES, male, late 30s–40s
PONY JONES, female, late 30s–40s

Setting

The play takes place in the present, in a regular and semi-rural town, not far from some mountains. The particular settings are:

The porch and backyard of Jennifer and Bob's house.

A grocery store.

The kitchen of Pony and John's house.

The backyard of Pony and John's house.

Note on the Text

Run-on sentences punctuated with commas are meant to represent speech as it's generally spoken. These may look ungrammatical but are entirely consistent with the way contemporary speech is generally spoken. There shouldn't be too many pauses or too much effort shown in changing the direction of the line, within the line, unless indicated.

Scene 1

Porch and backyard of Jennifer and Bob's modest house, late spring, late night. Silhouette of mountains in the background. Jennifer and Bob are seated at a picnic table, drinking water and tea. Bob looks as if he's trying to remember something. All is calm. An owl hoots, in the distance.

JENNIFER: I love that sound. *(Brief pause)* When was the last time we painted the house?

BOB: I don't know. It's probably years.

JENNIFER: Maybe we should do it over the summer.

BOB: Then wouldn't we just have to do it again?

JENNIFER: Isn't that what people do?

BOB: I guess.

JENNIFER: It's not some crazy theory. People paint their houses.

BOB: So then we'll paint the house.

JENNIFER: I think that'd be good. *(Brief pause)* It's going to be okay.

BOB: No, I know.

JENNIFER: You don't act like it. *(Brief pause)* It's such a pretty night. It's so quiet. You can almost hear the clouds go by.

BOB: Almost. *(Brief pause)* Remember the night I was, um— *(He feels a small sharp pain)* Auughh. *(He makes a quick adjustment to the way he's sitting)* That's better.

JENNIFER: Are you okay?

BOB: I was just sitting funny.

JENNIFER: I didn't think it was funny.

(Bob smiles. He glances at his watch. Brief pause.)

What night? Remember which night?

BOB: Oh, right. *(He tries to remember)* Nope. Totally gone.

JENNIFER: Clouds, beautiful nights?

BOB: Yeah, I know. *(Tries again)* Yeah, sorry. All gone.

JENNIFER: You've been doing that.

BOB: There hasn't been a lot of memorable stuff going on.

JENNIFER: Oh, is that it?

BOB *(Takes a sip of water)*: This glass tastes terrible.

JENNIFER: It's been sitting. *(Pause)* Do you want to talk?

BOB: What was just the whole thing about painting the house? And the other night about Belgium?

JENNIFER: That was two very short conversations. I don't have some particular, I'm not . . . it just seems like we don't talk.

BOB: What are we doing right now? Math?

JENNIFER: No, we're— I don't know— sort of throwing words at each other.

BOB: What? Come on, throwing . . . I thought we were just sitting here. But, fine, let's talk.

JENNIFER: Good. *(Brief pause)* What's the thing you're most, or just, what's your biggest fear?

BOB: My biggest? Like I have so many, they have to be ranked?

JENNIFER: I'm asking if there's something you're worried about.

BOB *(Sharply)*: I was just sitting here, you know, and now we're suddenly getting—

JENNIFER *(Interrupting)*: We're not suddenly anything. It's fine, we can just sit. *(Gently)* It really is a beautiful night. It's like that night when we— *(She is interrupted by the crash of metal garbage cans, offstage)* What was that?

BOB: Skunk. Maybe a raccoon.

JENNIFER: Should we look?

BOB: Yeah, but wait.

(They both listen. A shared but very subtle moment of excitement. She puts her hand on his.)

JENNIFER *(Quietly)*: The unknown.

BOB *(Agreeing quietly)*: I know.

(Some muffled offstage voices. John enters, finishing a conversation with Pony. He's holding a wrapped bottle of wine.)

JOHN: . . . but, yeah, it was definitely much more powerful when I was a kid. *(To Jennifer and Bob)* Hey, hi. Sorry. We heard you talking back here.

PONY: Very softly.

JOHN: Yeah. Sorry about the, um— that was your garbage cans. They almost had me. We just wanted to say hi. We brought you a little— well, I think it's obvious.

JENNIFER: Wow, thank you. Hi.

PONY: Hi. We're Pony and John. You must be the Joneses. It's on your mailbox. We're Joneses, too. We're renting the house at the end of the road with the blue shutters and the—

JOHN *(Interrupting)*: It's like two-hundred feet from here. It's right over there.

BOB: Sure, we know that house. Someone else used to live there.

JOHN: Wow. Who knew the place had such an interesting history.

PONY: Look at these salt and pepper shakers. Cute.

BOB *(Picking one up)*: These were made at a factory.

JENNIFER: Bob is filled with fun facts like that. *(To Pony and John)* Can you sit down?

JOHN: I practically invented sitting down. Actually, that's not true.

(Pony and John sit.)

PONY: It's so nice here. Our old town was built right on top of this huge leak of dry-cleaning chemicals.

JOHN: The leak happened later. I don't think they built the town on top of the leak.

PONY: Well, whichever— I think I was allergic. I'm just glad we're gone.

JENNIFER: How'd you end up deciding on here?

PONY: I always wanted to live in one of these little towns near the mountains. So, one night, he comes home and literally just says, literally . . . I forget what you said exactly.

JOHN: Just, something about moving to one of these little towns near the mountains.

PONY: That was it. It was all sort of a whirlwind.

JOHN: The time had come. *(Noticing a tiny white particle on Pony's sweater, he gently removes it, while speaking)* It's what my lady wanted. And what my lady wants, with some huge and basic exceptions, my lady gets. *(To Pony)* Styrofoam.

PONY: It's from that box. *(To Jennifer)* You must really like it, here. *(To John)* Is it still there?

JENNIFER: We do.

JOHN: I bet. *(To Pony, referring to Styrofoam)* No. All gone.

BOB: Moving is a pain.

JOHN: It is. Well said. Staying still is no picnic, either.

BOB: No.

JENNIFER: But here you are. I'm Jennifer, by the way.

PONY: My mom's name was Jennifer. Hi.

JENNIFER: Pony is a wonderful name.

PONY: My dad thought it up.

BOB: Well, it was already a word.

PONY: Yeah, but it didn't mean me. He said my arms and legs looked too long and weak. He's, um, he— *(She subtly and kind of lazily makes a throat-slitting gesture)*

JENNIFER: He was murdered?

PONY: No. God, no. But, thank you. *(Checking her sweater for bits of Styrofoam. To John)* Is there any more? I got inside the big box our TV was in. I was calling out, "I'm in the secret room."

JOHN: I started thinking, "Wow, this place has a secret room?" Then I heard you laughing. The whole box started shaking.

PONY: Then he tried climbing in with me.

JOHN: We were really laughing. *(Brief pause)* Yeah, that's it, that's the end of the story. Now you say something.

JENNIFER: Oh, okay. Let's see.

BOB: Bob.

PONY: What?

BOB: Did I say that before?

JENNIFER: His name is Bob. That sounds like a nice first day.

PONY: It was really good.

JOHN: We try to enjoy ourselves.

PONY: I'm sorry, can I use your bathroom?

JENNIFER: Sure. It's down the hall, on the left.

PONY: Thanks. *(She exits)*

BOB *(Pause. To Jennifer, as if to say, "I'm not going to start the conversation")*: Don't look at me.

JOHN: Yeah, don't look at him. No, I'm kidding— you can look at him. *(Looks around the yard and then up at the sky)* Do you guys know any of the constellations?

JENNIFER: I used to know some. Orion?

JOHN: Oh, yeah— where's that one?

JENNIFER: I just remember the name.

JOHN: Well, it's probably up there somewhere. *(Brief pause)* This is weird, sorry, but, do you have another bathroom?

JENNIFER: Ah, we do, actually. It's in the basement, bottom of the stairs.

JOHN: Don't get up. Bottom of the stairs. I'll find it. Thanks. Sorry. *(He exits)*

BOB *(Long still pause)*: Orion means "the bear."

JENNIFER: Isn't that *Ursa*? *Ursa Major*, the big bear?

BOB *(Looking toward the house)*: What are they doing in there?

JENNIFER: I would guess it's probably one of two things. It'll be nice to have someone over there.

BOB: I liked when it was empty.

JENNIFER: Yeah, that was a lot of fun, too.

PONY *(Pause. Enters)*: Hi, sorry. Where did— did John leave? Oh, no. Did he go?

JENNIFER: No, he's using the other bathroom. You think he would just leave?

PONY *(Sits down, next to Bob)*: No, of course not. I like that flower poster you have.

JENNIFER: Oh, in the bathroom, the print?

BOB: I used to stare at it when I was in there.

JENNIFER: And you don't anymore?

BOB: I probably still do. I think I used to generally stare more. These days, you know— no time. *(He picks a piece of lint off Pony's sweater)* Another piece.

PONY: I think John got it all.

JENNIFER: Yeah, Bob, maybe you should not touch our guests.

JOHN *(Enters)*: Whoa, what did I miss?

BOB: No, she had some . . . you didn't miss anything.

PONY *(To John)*: We left them all alone out here.

JOHN *(To Jennifer)*: Oh, my God— are you all right?

JENNIFER *(Amused)*: I'm fine.

BOB *(Perhaps feeling ganged up on)*: What's this, all of a sudden?

JOHN: That's exactly what I'm always saying. It should be on my gravestone. Or maybe just my name and dates, I don't know. *(To Bob)* We're not so different, you and me.

BOB: I think we're probably very different.

JOHN: Yeah, me too, actually.

JENNIFER *(She begins unwrapping the wine bottle. To Bob)*: Do you want to get some glasses?

BOB: I was kind of sitting, but—

JENNIFER *(Interrupting)*: I'll go.

BOB: No, I'll go. *(He exits)*

JENNIFER: This looks good.

PONY: It's from Europe.

JOHN: Just outside Europe. *(Very brief pause)* There was free iced tea where we had dinner.

JENNIFER: Do you want something different to drink?

JOHN: I was explaining the bathroom.

PONY: We probably drank a gallon each. I hope it doesn't keep me up.

JOHN: It's not the worst night for insomnia.

PONY: I hate insomnia. I don't even like saying it.

JOHN: You'll sleep. It's a pretty night is all I meant.

JENNIFER: I was just saying that to Bob. *(A quieter voice)* He's, um, the last few months, he's ill. So we're just kind of laying low and trying to figure that out.

PONY: What's there to figure out?

JENNIFER: Well, plenty, actually. They keep changing the treatment and the drugs. But you have a point.

PONY: What does he, I mean, is it contagious?

JENNIFER: It's most likely congenital. It's very rare.

PONY: So, I'm sorry, so it's not?

JENNIFER: No. They don't know much about it. There's a chance it's more popular. I mean, common.

PONY: I hope he's, wow, yeah—

JENNIFER: Well, we do too— thank you. One of the best doctors for his thing is right here in town. Actually, the best.

JOHN: Yeah?

JENNIFER: And there's a patient of his, Elliot, and I talk with him and his wife to get a sense of how the disease, just, how it goes from month to month. It's interesting, he's an albino, Elliot, which I always thought was interesting. But it's, um, it's hard, it's really . . . yeah.

PONY: Say no more.

JENNIFER: Have you had experience with something like this?

PONY: I just didn't want you to say any more.

JENNIFER: No, of course— Bob doesn't like talking about it, either. In fact, we kind of distinctly never do.

JOHN: Then let's do that.

JENNIFER: I'm sorry. I just kind of blurted all that out.

JOHN: That's all right. That's what separates us from the animal. You never hear animals blurting things out. Unless they're being run over by a car or something.

(Bob enters, with a glass of water and no wine glasses.)

JENNIFER: Did you bring the . . . *(Bob turns and exits)*
PONY *(To John)*: That's like you.
JOHN: Sometimes, I forget stuff. On the other hand, sometimes I remember stuff.
JENNIFER: So, wow— you can do it all. *(John smiles)* We had a leak in the roof, almost a year ago, and everything is still kind of musty. So we like to sit out here.
JOHN: Nothing wrong with any of that.
PONY *(Picking up a CD audiobook from the table)*: Is this any good? "Every House Is a Halfway House."
JENNIFER: It's supposed to be a memoir. We never listened. Those are from, Bob had trouble with his vision, a few months ago. I mean, he couldn't see. I got some audiobooks, because I thought it'd be nice to listen to a story, but then he just got better.
PONY: Does he work with, like, insulation and heating stuff?
JENNIFER: No. Why?
PONY: Because John just had that, for a few days.
JOHN: Guilty. Actually, guilty's not what I mean— I just couldn't see anything.
PONY: It turned out it was from this material they used to use inside wood stoves.
JENNIFER: Really? No, this was nothing like that. It was called cortical blindness, and it comes from high blood pressure. Bob thought it was from a dinner I made. So now he's never eating artichokes again. It's scary, though. Losing your eyesight. I mean, I imagine.
JOHN: Yeah. It's highly personal, going blind.
PONY: It was only a few days. Thank God.

JOHN *(Picking up the audiobook)*: I found this company that'll send you the transcript of any audiobook.

JENNIFER *(Brief pause)*: Wouldn't that just be the book?

JOHN: You know what, you're right. That would just be the book.

PONY *(To John)*: Afterward, remember? *(To Jennifer)* He went into kind of a thing.

JENNIFER: What do you mean?

JOHN: I guess I was trying to—

PONY *(Interrupting)*: Just, he wouldn't eat, wouldn't sleep. You were really weird.

JENNIFER: Well, you were probably pretty shaken up. *(Bob returns with wine glasses)*

JOHN: I probably was.

PONY: Then he went down to the ocean. *(To John)* You said you wanted to be near something really vast.

JENNIFER: Vast.

PONY: That was his exact words. *(Brief pause)* I wasn't very supportive. I'm just not, I mean, that whole stuff . . . luckily we had a good neighbor.

JOHN: No, come on, you were great.

JENNIFER: What whole stuff?

JOHN: People getting moody and going blind. It's just not really her thing. *(To Pony)* Not your thang.

PONY *(To John)*: It really isn't my thang. *(Brief pause)* When you took that trip, I thought you were leaving me. I thought he was leaving.

JOHN: But I wasn't. Or, I was, and I didn't do a very good job at it. *(Brief pause. To Bob)* The topic is: things that have happened.

BOB: I can see wanting to go down by the ocean.

JENNIFER: You don't even know what we're talking about.

BOB: Well, whatever you're talking about, I can see wanting to go down to the ocean. Being near something vast.

JOHN: See? He knows.

BOB: Where'd you go, exactly?

JOHN: I guess about a week and half.

BOB: I said, where.

PONY: The ocean. It seemed like a year. When you got back is when we started talking about moving.

JENNIFER: Pony, what do you do?

PONY: I have a greeting card business? It's mostly online, so I can do it from anywhere. I could also not do it from anywhere, and, that'd be fine, too. But it's good, it pays some bills.

JOHN *(Very brief pause. To Pony)*: I think she meant, like, hobbies.

JENNIFER: No, that's what I was asking. And how about you?

JOHN: For work? Space program. Astronaut.

JENNIFER: You're kidding. That's amazing.

JOHN: Well, I use the term loosely.

JENNIFER: I didn't know the term could be used loosely. But still.

JOHN: I know. Still.

PONY: I never know what he's talking about. Say one of your things.

JOHN *(Very brief pause)*: Oh, this is a good one. So, if you take the letters from the words "The United States of America," and you scramble them all up, it doesn't spell anything. It's just gobbledygook, total nonsense.

PONY: See?

BOB: So don't scramble them up.

JOHN: Actually, that's not a bad idea.

BOB: She asked what you do for work.

JOHN: Heating and air-conditioning.

JENNIFER: Oh, nice.

JOHN: I got some part-time work and I'm going to try to pick up some jobs on the side. What about yourself?

JENNIFER: Well, a job is a job.

JOHN: Wrong! No, you're right.

JENNIFER: Okay. But, so, anyway, I do bookkeeping for a couple of businesses in town. And Bob works for the Department of Transportation. He does all the ordering, like for paint and signposts. Don't you, Bob?

BOB *(Brief pause)*: What do you want me to say?

JENNIFER: How about, "Yes."

BOB: Yes.

PONY: It's funny, all that paint on the road—I never thought about who orders it. Do they ever use something other than yellow for the lines in the middle?

BOB: No, but, actually, do you know why those lines are always yellow?

PONY: No, why?

BOB: I think somebody just picked it a long time ago.

PONY: Oh.

JOHN: It's exciting to get the inside story.

PONY *(To Bob)*: You seem fine.

BOB: You too.

PONY *(Stands, looking around the yard)*: Does the yard go all the way around?

BOB: It just goes back around there a little. You should do modeling. *(Brief pause, as Jennifer and John look at Bob)* No, I mean, just, everyone should. Everyone should do modeling. *(Brief pause)* I'm on leave, right now. Taking some time off.

JENNIFER: We used to never see each other, we were both so busy. I used to never be able to hear who Bob thought should do modeling.

PONY *(Brief pause)*: John, look. *(She shows him her hand. A tiny, practically invisible bruise)*

JOHN: It looks better.

PONY: I closed a drawer on my thumb.

BOB: Ouch.

PONY *(With surprise)*: That's exactly what I said.

JOHN: It sort of says it all, doesn't it. *(Brief pause)* It really is quiet. You really *can* almost hear the clouds go by. *(Very brief pause)* We were listening in on you guys, earlier.

PONY: Not in a weird way.

JENNIFER: Oh, good.

PONY: Yeah, we were just standing over there in the dark, totally still.

JOHN: It sounds worse when you put it into words.

BOB: Everyone should try modeling, if they want. Or any occupation. That's all I was saying.

(Distant church bells ring.)

PONY: Listen to that, John. It's like a real place.

JOHN: Yeah. It just makes you feel right in the middle of the whole lonesome thing.

JENNIFER: What do you mean, lonesome?

JOHN: I don't know.

PONY: He meant something better.

JOHN: We heard an owl or something, earlier.

JENNIFER: I heard that! I see him every once in a while. He has these huge whooshing wings.

PONY: Nature was definitely one of the big selling points of here. Plus, the school system's supposed to be good.

JENNIFER: Oh, do you have kids?

PONY: No, it's just, John hates stupid children.

JOHN: I was under a lot of stress when I said that.

JENNIFER: The schools are supposed to be pretty good. *(Brief pause)* I love this time of night.

JOHN: Me too. What's out there, you know? What's it waiting to do?

PONY: You don't have to make it into some, like, make it be all scary.

JOHN: I'm not. There's things out there, is all I'm saying.

PONY *(Brief pause. To Bob)*: You got very quiet.

BOB: Well, you know what they say about still waters.

JOHN *(Very brief pause)*: Mosquitoes? Malaria?

JENNIFER *(With a smile)*: I think he means: they run deep.

JOHN: Okay, but, we both have a point.

JENNIFER *(To Bob)*: You are kind of still waters. But we communicate pretty well, even without words.

BOB *(Somewhat sharply)*: Yeah?

JOHN *(Brief pause. Looking at Bob's wristwatch)*: Is that the real time?

BOB *(Somewhat indignant: "Of course it's the real time.")*: This is a watch.

JENNIFER: So, you're all moved in?

JOHN: Pretty much. *(Responding to something he senses going on with Pony)* What?

PONY: Nothing, I was, just— I like it here.

JOHN: We'll be really happy here, Pony.

BOB: It's a nice area. You have to leave so I can go to bed.

JENNIFER: Bob's been taking a Toastmaster's class. Anyway, we should head in. But this'll make a good story some day. *(To John)* We thought you were a raccoon or a skunk, some crazy nighttime animal.

JOHN *(An almost proud smile)*: Yeah, nope. Sorry about that. My night vision was really good when I was a kid. *(Brief pause)* Actually, wait.

(All remain still and listen.)

BOB: What are we listening for?

(John puts a finger to his lips, as if to say, "Quiet.")

PONY *(Quietly)*: John's been reading a book about great mysteries of the world.

JOHN *(Still listening intently. Quietly)*: It's a magazine.

BOB *(Brief pause)*: It's really late.

JOHN *(He listens, intently, for a few more seconds, then, suddenly)*: It is pretty late. Well, it was nice meeting you guys. It's funny. The new neighbors move in. It's, like, the world's oldest profession.

BOB: What?

JOHN: I mean, the greatest story ever told. Oldest, I mean.

PONY: John and words—forget about it.

JENNIFER: I think you have a nice way with words.

JOHN *(Irish accent)*: Do you, now?

PONY: This was really nice. It's almost— *(She moves away, having spotted something underneath a chair or table)* Oh my God.

JOHN: What?

PONY: There's an animal or something.

JENNIFER: It's a squirrel. I don't think it's . . . *(Moving closer. She pokes it with a large barbecue spatula)* Yeah, it's all right, it's dead.

PONY: It's not all right.

BOB *(Having moved away, he stands near Pony)*: We should call Animal Control. *(Jennifer begins to pick it up with the spatula)* No, don't touch it.

JOHN: What are you going to do with that—flip it over?

JENNIFER: There's plastic bags under there.

BOB: This is why we don't have people over.

JENNIFER: *This* is why?

JOHN: I wonder why he picked here. Not that your patio isn't a great place to die.

PONY *(Looking in the other direction)*: You should call the fire department and have them spray at it.

BOB *(To Pony)*: I'm sorry about this.

PONY *(To John)*: Put it, throw it in the thing.

(John puts the dead squirrel in a dark plastic bag, which he keeps holding.)

JENNIFER *(Pointing to a small garbage can)*: That's garbage, right behind you.

JOHN *(Looking into the bag)*: And off you go, into the great oak tree in the sky, where there's no such thing as Jack Russell terriers or angry teenagers with—

BOB *(Interrupting)*: Would you just throw it away. *(John does so)*

JENNIFER: Well. That was . . . sorry . . . Phew. *(Very brief pause)* It'll be nice to have another girl around here. *(A very small shrug from Pony)* It was good meeting you both.

JOHN: Yeah, you too. Nice work. This was fun. *(To Bob, clarifying)* I mean, not fun, but, definitely some other word.

PONY: Definitely.

JOHN *(Very brief pause)*: Well, when the dead squirrel gets thrown away, that's usually our cue to head on home.

(To Bob) Don't look so sad. You'll live. *(He moves to put an arm around Pony, who recoils, in a not unloving way)*

PONY: I need to take a shower. You have to wash your hands. Bye. Sorry. I just wasn't expecting that. Or I guess I was expecting that there wasn't going to be that.

JOHN: It's sad, isn't it. His little eyes, and the little paws. Running around, collecting acorns. "I'm a squirrel, I'm a squirrel." I'd love to say something in Latin, right now. *(To Bob)* You know what I mean, big guy?

BOB: I don't.

JOHN *(To Pony)*: All right, beautiful. Let's go back to the new place.

PONY *(Remembering and brightening, a little)*: "The new place." I like that. Bye.

(Pony and John exit, muffled conversation.)

JENNIFER: Bye. Oh, we never had the wine. Thank you. *(Long pause)* Well, wow . . . *(Brief pause)* They were certainly . . . did you like them? *(Bob nods, noncommittally)* They seem nice.

BOB: She seemed to like the yard. *(Brief pause)* Look how much I'm shaking.

JENNIFER: I don't see any . . . is it doing it?

BOB: No, it stopped. *(He stands and moves to the door)*

JENNIFER: It was nice watching you with people.

BOB: I wasn't any different. Are you coming in?

JENNIFER: Do you want me to? *(Brief pause)* I'm just going to sit here and listen for a while.

BOB: All right. *(Very brief pause. Standing in the doorway, behind the screen door)* It was nice watching you with people, too. You have a pretty smile.

JENNIFER: Oh, Bob. Just when I think you're not going to—

(We see Bob flick a switch as he exits the doorway. All light goes to black.)

Scene 2

Grocery store. John is eating some free cracker samples at a card table at the end of an aisle. Grocery store Muzak is playing. Jennifer enters with a purse and a plastic drugstore bag.

JOHN: Well, hey, if it isn't you.

JENNIFER: No, it is. Hi.

JOHN: I'm just saying, you know, what if it wasn't?

JENNIFER: Okay. John, right?

JOHN: Yeah. I supposedly had some work here, working on a freezer.

JENNIFER: But you don't?

JOHN: I guess they already got it fixed. They only called about it yesterday or the day before.

JENNIFER: Well, it's a freezer.

JOHN: Yes, it is. I messed up. Pony's coming to get me, later. This took a lot less time than I had originally estimated.

JENNIFER: What did, doing nothing?

JOHN: Yeah. Wait, I love this part. *(He points toward the source of the Muzak, and they listen for a second)* That wasn't it, actually. So, what are you doing?

JENNIFER: Just errands. I had to pick up some stuff for Bob. I think I told you guys about his—yeah, I told you.

JOHN: You did, yeah. *(He sits on the edge of the wobbly card table)*

JENNIFER: Is that a good place to sit?

JOHN: Totally.

JENNIFER: Okay. Well, I have to get some things here.

JOHN: What do you have to get?

JENNIFER: Groceries.

JOHN: Oh my God, I love groceries. *(Standing, referring to the card table)* Actually, you're right, this is really wobbly.

JENNIFER: Well, I'll see you later.

JOHN: It's weird. You want this conversation to end, but, I want it to keep going.

JENNIFER: That is weird.

JOHN: I know. I saw you before. A few weeks ago, out in the parking lot. You were on the phone, crying, and eating a power bar. I thought, wow, that's one sad busy person.

JENNIFER: Oh. When were you here, a few weeks ago? I thought you just moved here.

JOHN: Oh, we did, but, yeah, I had told Pony I was at the ocean.

JENNIFER: Okay.

JOHN: It's actually sort of ironic.

JENNIFER *(Brief pause)*: Are you . . . I thought you were going to expand on that.

JOHN: No, I think that was it.

JENNIFER: I should really get—

JOHN *(Interrupting)*: Going, you want to get going. I know. So don't we all. I don't know what your normal look is. I mean, when you're okay.

JENNIFER: Why, how do I seem? I probably look like I'm, like . . .

JOHN *(Brief pause)*: You don't have to say anything.

JENNIFER: I know. I like when they put out free samples.

JOHN: As do I.

JENNIFER: This has been such a . . . I brought Bob a coffee, this morning, and he spilled it all over himself.

JOHN: Is he all right?

JENNIFER: He's okay. But he never, just, he didn't do anything. Boiling hot coffee, all down his front. Then he said, "It smells like work."

JOHN: He was probably in shock.

JENNIFER: He didn't even flinch. And then he just stared at me. I have no idea what he was thinking.

JOHN: He was probably thinking all kinds of things. *(Brief pause)* I have a great flinch. Watch this. *(He demonstrates a tiny flinch)* See? Just very subtle, it's almost classical. *(Brief pause)* No, but mornings are tough.

JENNIFER: It's not mornings. It's one of the stages and the stages don't go backward. Copper starts building up in the blood— which, that's just one of the problems. And then this thing starts called "sensual mortification." Isn't that an awful phrase? But you never know what's a sign of what, because things get bad and things get better. They talk about symptoms being "sluggish" and "seething." There's this whole awful vocabulary. Bob has something called Harriman Leavey syndrome.

JOHN: It sounds like a jazz combo.

JENNIFER: It isn't. It's just the name of the person who discovered it, and then, syndrome. *(Brief pause)* Do you do other kinds of work, other than refrigerators?

JOHN: That's not something I really need to talk about. Unless you need some work done?

JENNIFER: No. We're thinking about painting the house.

JOHN: Well, make sure you pick a color you like. Anyway, go on— you were talking about Bob's thing, the Benny Goodman Experience.

JENNIFER: It's the Harriman Leavey syndrome. It's an irreversible and degenerative nerve disease. Do you have a hilarious punchline for that?

JOHN: No. Actually, wait. *(He may have thought of a punchline)* No, that wouldn't work. *(Very brief pause)* I'm sorry, go ahead. I'll listen.

JENNIFER: I don't talk to anybody about this. *(Very brief pause)* So, yeah, now he's doing this treatment, which is, just, the AMA doesn't recognize it because there isn't a whole protocol, yet. It's hard, because he never . . . I mean, Bob doesn't want to know anything about any of it. He keeps saying, "Just tell me where to be and what to take."

JOHN: I could understand that.

JENNIFER: I don't know if you could.

JOHN: Probably not. Did you hear me listening, just then?

JENNIFER: Oh, is that what that was.

JOHN: The secret is not saying anything.

JENNIFER: That's, yeah, that's actually pretty good advice about listening. The doctor says it's probably good for us to keep it simple and just have a positive attitude. *(Referring to the bag)* This is supposed to reduce the copper uptake. It builds up in the brain. Mainly in the language centers.

JOHN: The language centers— yowza. Watch out for oysters and liver.

JENNIFER: I know. They're really high in copper. Why do you know that?

JOHN: I do work for a lot of hospitals and clinics. On my breaks, I usually read those medical journals. Just to see what's out there.

JENNIFER: What else have you read? What do they say about treatments?

JOHN: I stopped reading. At a certain point you just stop and say— I don't know, probably different people stop and say different things.

JENNIFER: This all started when Bob was filling out some thing for a raffle to win a trip to Canada. I thought he was having a stroke. He kept saying, "How do you say our address?"

JOHN: Oww.

JENNIFER: We used to travel. I have a picture of us on camels. Just in Texas, but still.

JOHN *(Very brief pause)*: So is he taking other stuff, other than the stuff for copper?

JENNIFER: Oh, God, the drugs are a whole other thing. Some people have a negative reaction that seems like a positive change. So it's just all these different levels of not knowing anything.

JOHN: There's a lot to not know, isn't there.

JENNIFER: Yeah, there is.

JOHN: You have a lot of composure.

JENNIFER: Thank you.

JOHN: Oh, you took that as a compliment— okay.

JENNIFER: How did you mean it?

JOHN: Like you took it, however you took it.

JENNIFER: You seem kind of committed to not being sympathetic.

JOHN: That isn't what I'm trying not to be.

JENNIFER: If you say so. There's a guy I always see at the clinic.

JOHN: The albino guy.

JENNIFER: I told you this.

JOHN: No.

JENNIFER: He's in a wheelchair and he's always asking what just happened. He's always saying, "Did something just happen?" Today, I was thinking, "Is that Bob, tomorrow? Bob, next year?" I don't know how everybody does this.

JOHN: Yeah.

JENNIFER *(Brief pause)*: I studied Italian in school.

JOHN: Say something Italian.

JENNIFER: You have to speak it all the time.

JOHN: Yeah. *(He gently grasps her arm, at the bicep)*

JENNIFER: What are you doing?

JOHN: I don't know. Reaching out.

JENNIFER: Why?

JOHN: Because. And because you have pretty eyes. They're sad, but they're pretty.

JENNIFER: Well, that's very— I actually need glasses to read.

JOHN: Interesting.

JENNIFER: Is this what you do, comment on women?

JOHN: It's one of my things.

JENNIFER: I'm married.

JOHN: Who isn't.

JENNIFER: I don't know why I'm still standing here.

JOHN: Me neither. This might not be what it seems like.

JENNIFER: So, is this, are you making fun of me?

JOHN: No. *(He gently lets go of her arm)* I just was, you know, holding on to you.

JENNIFER: This isn't a good day, okay?

JOHN: No, of course not.

JENNIFER: I'm sure I just look like a person in a store.

JOHN: You don't look like a person in a store.

JENNIFER: I really try. With Bob. To just be there.

JOHN: Yeah. *(Brief pause. With understanding)* It's not the greatest name, is it.

JENNIFER: Which? Bob? You're criticizing my husband's name?

JOHN: Someone had to.

JENNIFER: I'm not sure that's true. I always liked it.

JOHN: Okay.

JENNIFER: I did. "Bob." It's easy to remember. I think dyslexics find it comforting. *(Brief pause)* Do my eyes really look sad?

JOHN: No. A little. *(Very brief pause)* Don't say anything to Pony, okay?

JENNIFER: About what?

JOHN: Maybe, to be safe, about anything. Just never say a single word to her, about any topic.

JENNIFER *(They share a tiny smile)*: Okay.

JOHN: Thanks.

JENNIFER *(Very brief pause)*: I love my husband.

JOHN: Oh my God, who doesn't? Listen, I should get out front, but, here's a little haiku:

The frog is dark green.
He is breathing like crazy.
It's starting to snow.

JENNIFER *(Brief pause)*: I don't know if a haiku is the best way
to end a conversation.

JOHN: No, I'm sure it isn't. But, hey, I'll see you later.

(Lights down.)

Scene 3

Daytime. Pony and John's kitchen. John is sitting, re-wiring a lamp. A small pile of magazines and pamphlets sits near him on the floor. There's no kitchen table. Pony is in workout clothing.

PONY: I'm home!

JOHN: Me too. *(Referring to the lamp)* Can you believe someone threw this out?

PONY: Does it work?

JOHN: No.

PONY: Then, yes. We need to get a table.

JOHN *(Distracted)*: That, I'll admit.

PONY *(Goes to get something from the refrigerator and recoils and closes the door)*: Sweetie, yuck. It still smells like something.

JOHN: Everything smells like something.

PONY: It should just smell like cold air and plastic.

JOHN *(Referring to a little mark on her sweatshirt)*: There's something on your sweatshirt.

PONY *(Looking at it)*: No, that's from, these kids were sitting near the running track, flicking lit matches around. I was daring them to see if they could leave a mark.

JOHN: While you were wearing it?

PONY: They were just kids.

JOHN: Oh, good— then I don't have any more questions about that.

PONY: Maybe next time you can go with me. Hey, what was "nickels," last night?

JOHN: What?

PONY: You were yelling "nickels" in your sleep.

JOHN: Oh, yeah. Dr. Nichols. She was our doctor when I was little.

PONY: And now you're yelling her name in the night?

JOHN: Are you mad at me for having a bad dream?

PONY: No. We need a new shower curtain.

JOHN: We'll make a list.

PONY: I don't want to turn into those guys, next door.

JOHN: How do you mean?

PONY: Just, like, "Oh, hi—my name is Bob and Jennifer."

JOHN: Yeah, I don't think we're going to start saying that. *(He picks up a sponge and a spray bottle)* Now, you sit there and look beautiful and completely impossible and I'll do this.

PONY: I'm not impossible. *(She picks up the pile of pamphlets and begins looking through them, as he attends to the fridge)* I tried with that pine-scented stuff but now it just smells like a Christmas tree with garbage in it.

JOHN: Ah, that sends me back.

(John sticks his head in the fridge, opens a drawer, removes a small leaky bag of produce and carries it outside.)

PONY: Was that in the drawer? Uggh. I didn't want to even look. *(She returns to leafing through pamphlets and brochures. He continues cleaning)* I want to start using dandelions in salads.

JOHN: No, you don't.

PONY: What are all these pamphlets?

JOHN: I love pamphlets.

PONY *(She looks at one)*: Why are you reading about meditation?

JOHN: I don't know, I've been thinking about it. *(Very brief pause. A dizzy spell/episode)* Whoa. God.

PONY: What?

JOHN: Nothing. I just, wow, I just inhaled a ton of ammonia.

PONY: Oh, honey, don't do that.

JOHN: You should've told me that twenty seconds ago.

PONY: Are you okay?

JOHN: Wow. Yeah.

PONY: Be careful. *(Looking at the cleaning supplies)* Wait, that's ammonia. What've you been using?

JOHN: Whatever this is.

PONY *(She glances at the spray bottle)*: I don't think that's anything. I think it's just water.

JOHN: Oh, yeah. It smelled weird, at first. *(Brief pause)* Read me something.

PONY *(Reading)*: "Calligraphy: Is it just for wedding invitations."

JOHN: I read that one. Little spoiler alert: It can actually be used for other things.

PONY *(Picks up another brochure)*: "Great Meadows Community College: Where little acorns become"—wait, is this a typo?—"Where little acorns become big acorns."

JOHN: I think the sports teams are called The Acorns.

PONY: It's still not a very good motto.

JOHN: I thought we could take a class. Cooking or something.

PONY: That'd be fun. *(Looking at another pamphlet)* What's "Harriman Leavey syndrome."

JOHN: Nothing. I was working at some clinic.

PONY: You've been getting a lot of work.

JOHN: Not really. I'm doing a lot of estimates, though.

PONY: How'd that freezer thing go?

JOHN: What?

PONY: The grocery store.

JOHN: Oh, it was good.

PONY: We have to figure out the car situation.

JOHN: We will.

PONY *(Reading)*: "'This thing, and it's fair to call it a thing, is energetic, elusive, and highly mortal,' says Dr. Harriman Leavey, who is also an amateur cellist." My cousin played cello. She almost went to England for it.

JOHN: Everything is mortal.

PONY: Not everything is everything.

JOHN: Then what is it, then?

PONY *(Pulling a thread off her shirt)*: Get off of there, you. *(Still looking at the pamphlet. Reading, absentmindedly)* "Palliative."

JOHN *(Brief pause. Sporadically returns to fixing the lamp)*: Hey, I have to tell you something. This is stupid. I didn't do that freezer job.

PONY: Oh. Why'd you say you did?

JOHN: I was embarrassed I screwed up.

PONY: You don't ever lie.

JOHN: I know.

PONY: My dad always said, "I don't need you to tell the truth, just don't lie."

JOHN: I know. You've told me that. So, are we all right?

PONY: I am. *(Begins reading another pamphlet)* Hey, there's an apple orchard around here.

JOHN: I thought you'd like that. *(He stands. He checks his pulse at the neck)*

PONY: They have mini-golf. What?

JOHN: Nothing. Stood up too quick. *(Makes finishing touches on the wiring job)* There we go. *(He plugs it in. Turns it on. It doesn't work)* Huh.

PONY: Can you believe someone threw that out?

JOHN: Yeah, yeah. *(Brief pause)* Don't ask kids to flick lit matches at you, okay?

PONY: If that's so important to you, you should've told me, before.

JOHN: I thought I did.

PONY *(Sensing something having changed in John)*: What?

JOHN: I said, nothing.

(Lights down.)

Scene 4

Jennifer and Bob's backyard and porch. Morning, bright sunshine.
Bob is sitting at the picnic table.

JENNIFER *(Enters, with coffee for Bob)*: Be careful. Are you
   ready? We're almost late.

BOB: It's impossible to be almost late.

JENNIFER: I'd love to hear more about that, Bob, but, come on,
   we're almost late.

BOB *(Checks his pockets)*: Have you seen my keys?

JENNIFER: I have mine.

BOB: Let me just look.

JENNIFER: Bob, we're late.

BOB: I, just, I want to have my keys. People carry keys.

JENNIFER: Me, for instance. Come on, let's go, we don't need
   two. We're not launching nuclear missiles.

BOB: I feel like I'm just staying at someone's house.

JENNIFER: Okay, we'll find your keys. *(Begins to look)*

BOB: You don't have to do everything, you know.

JENNIFER: God, what do you want me to do, Bob?

BOB: I can do things. It's like you need me to be helpless. I never asked you to leave work.

JENNIFER: I'm going to take a little breath here— I don't want to get upset. *(She takes a breath)* Huh, that didn't do anything. I am really fucking upset, Bob. You distinctly asked me, begged me practically, to leave work so I could be with you, so I could be by your side.

BOB: I know.

JENNIFER: And you won't hear a single word about any of it. "I don't need the details, I just want to get better."

BOB: I do want to get better.

JENNIFER: Me too. I'm in this with you. But it's like someone saying, "Yeah, sure, I'll marry you, but, after that, leave me alone."

BOB: It's not like that. I wasn't trying to make you mad.

JENNIFER: No? What were you trying to make me? Hurt? Sad?

BOB: No.

JENNIFER: Let's go.

BOB *(Finds the keys in his pocket)*: Here they are.

JENNIFER: Who would've thought.

BOB: Don't make fun of me. I thought I'd checked.

JENNIFER *(Brief pause)*: I'm trying as hard as I can. As much as I can.

BOB: I know. *(Brief pause)* Maybe it'd be easier if just you went. Since I'm making you mad.

JENNIFER: What?

BOB: Now that we're talking about it, maybe I should stay. It's just hearing a bunch of numbers.

JENNIFER: You have to be kidding me.

BOB: Going over there makes me feel like I'm sick.

JENNIFER: Me too. But, you are sick, Bob.

BOB: That's not all I am. And I'm going to get over it.

JENNIFER: Well, this seems like a whole other conversation, and now we're late. *I'm* late, I guess.

BOB: It'll be all right. He always makes you wait, once you get there. Can you tell him there was a little more blood?

JENNIFER: When?

BOB: Last night and just now.

JENNIFER: No, Bob, you should come, just come with me, and you can sit in the car. So if he needs to see you, we don't have to keep making trips.

BOB: Okay.

JENNIFER: How much? What did it look like?

BOB: Just red. Red and yellow.

JENNIFER: Okay, well, let's go. Maybe it's the medication, again.

BOB: That's what I was thinking.

JENNIFER: We can sit by the lake, on the way back.

BOB: That might be good.

JENNIFER: If you want. *(Sound of a hot-air balloon approaching; that is, the periodic sound of the burner. Looking up)* Oh, look. I forgot. They're having that balloon festival, this weekend. God. Wouldn't you love to go up in one of those?

BOB *(Also looking up)*: And just kind of float above it all? No.

JENNIFER *(Still looking up at the balloon moving past)*: It must be so quiet when it isn't noisy.

BOB: I don't see why they have to be such bright colors.

JENNIFER: They're hot-air balloons, Bob.

BOB: Understood. It just seems like a lot of color. *(Very brief pause)* We should get going.

(He exits. Jennifer looks at the balloons for a moment, grabs Bob's coffee cup, then exits.
Lights down.)

Scene 5

Daytime. Pony and John's kitchen. Pony is seated at their new kitchen table, which is clearly used, doing some paperwork, looking through some catalogs related to her greeting card business, checking something on her laptop computer, etc. John enters, fills a coffee mug with water, adds some instant drink mix.

PONY: People don't really send greeting cards, anymore.

JOHN: You always sell some in the wintertime, though.

PONY: I should do something else. *(Referring to his instant drink)* That stuff is gross.

JOHN: The drink I'm about to enjoy, right now? Yeah.

PONY: I wish I drank coffee.

JOHN: Why?

PONY: Because then I'd have a coffee. And I'd go, "Mmm. This is good coffee," and I'd look out a window. And I'd be somebody else.

JOHN: So start drinking coffee.

PONY *(Brief pause)*: It seems like you're rustling around, every night.

JOHN: Am I waking you up?

PONY: No, but can you do your breathing somewhere else?

JOHN: What?

PONY: Whatever you're doing in the bathroom. It's like panting or something.

JOHN: Oh. Sorry. Yeah— it's this deep-breathing thing. I didn't think you heard that.

PONY: I do. It sounds like you're crying.

JOHN: Come on— do I look like someone who leans on the sink and cries all night? *(Brief pause)* No, it's for relaxation.

PONY: What do you need to relax about? Me?

JOHN: No, come on. Just, moving, work, just life.

PONY: You don't care about that stuff.

JOHN: I know.

PONY: I can do it with you, if you want. The exercises. *(Brief pause)* That pottery studio had a sign out front for an apprentice.

JOHN: That'd be fun. Pottery's great. *(Holds up his coffee mug)* This thing is pottery.

PONY: Could we not talk about pottery, for one second? *(Brief pause)* I always think a different place is going to feel different.

JOHN: Yeah.

PONY: I feel like I should go to med school or get my hair cut or something.

JOHN: I know.

PONY: That's all you're going to say?

JOHN: Okay, come on, let's see you smile.

PONY *(She doesn't smile)*: I'm not good at anything.

JOHN *(Very brief pause)*: Where's that smile.

PONY *(She doesn't smile)*: So, there was this guy in a wheelchair out in front of the post office, this morning. When I walked past, he said, "Is it just me?" And then he started trying to yell. I could still see him, when I was in line. Then an ambulance came. I was trying not to look.

JOHN: What was wrong with him?

PONY: It might've been the guy Jennifer was talking about, the other night. He was totally pale, like, bright white, even his eyelashes. He was like a ghost.

JOHN *(Comforts her with a hand on her shoulder)*: I'm sorry, sweetie. You weren't expecting that.

PONY: Do you know what I thought the whole time? I just wanted to watch TV with you.

JOHN: Aww, Pony.

PONY: I did. I wished we were watching that show about antiques. I just wanted to be making our funny comments at the television.

JOHN: It's a good show for that.

PONY: I like the people way in the background, walking by and looking at the camera, trying to carry all their crazy stuff. Remember that guy with the fake violin? He got so mad.

JOHN: I thought he was going to hit the lady who told him, the way he was yelling. He had a point though. A hundred-year-old fake is still a real antique.

PONY: Remember we saw him in the background, later? Like he was trying to get second opinions from everyone.

JOHN: It was hard not to feel for that guy. I was able to do it, but, it was hard.

BOB *(Appears at the screen door)*: Hi.

PONY: Hey, Bob.

BOB: Hi. This is nice. The screen. *(Brief pause)* What's that?

JOHN: No one said anything.

BOB: Okay. Do you have any sugar?

PONY: Seriously? You're here to borrow sugar?

BOB: Jennifer's at the store. *(Brief pause)* Have a good one. *(Exits)*

PONY: Didn't you want— *(Calling to him)* I think we do have some sugar. *(No response)* That was weird. What's going on with him?

JOHN: Hard to tell. *(Brief pause)* Maybe he just wanted some sugar.

(Lights down.)

Scene 6

Porch and backyard of Jennifer and Bob's house. Late at night. Mostly darkness. Jennifer is seated in the lawn, having a glass of wine, looking up. Indirect light and muffled sound of a very humble fireworks display, accompanied by low sound of a recording of Eastern chanting or Tuvan throat-singing. Bob appears, and stands in the doorway.

JENNIFER: Hey. I didn't see you there.

BOB: Yup. I'm here. Weird music.

JENNIFER: I like it.

BOB: It's weird. They shouldn't be lighting fireworks.

JENNIFER: They're pretty. Do you want to come out?

BOB: I can see.

(The last muffled explosion of a firework.)

JENNIFER: Have you taken your stuff?

BOB: Can you remind me?

JENNIFER: Yeah. Come on out. *(He comes out and stands by Jennifer)* Do you want to sit? Do you want some wine?

BOB: I thought he said no alcohol.

JENNIFER: He just said moderation. *(The music stops)*

BOB: I should stop with coffee.

JENNIFER: That was so scary, Bob. The other morning.

BOB: That was pretty clumsy. *(Brief pause)* I know you've had to handle a lot. I'd do the same for you. You know that.

JENNIFER: I wouldn't want the same. I'd probably want to know every, I mean, all the risks and names and details.

BOB: Well, we're different. It just makes it easier.

JENNIFER *(Brief pause)*: I think about you.

BOB: God, can we— I hate when you say stuff like that.

JENNIFER: I said I think about you. You hate that? It's like the tiniest saddest little thing.

BOB: I'm sorry. Just, what am I supposed to say back?

JENNIFER: I don't know. "I think about *you.*" There's probably a million things. You just don't have to yell at me.

BOB: I didn't yell.

JENNIFER: I wish you would yell, sometimes.

BOB: Do you want me to yell or not yell?

JENNIFER: These are my two choices? *(Brief pause)* It's like you even want me to be scared for you. It's like you hate me because—

BOB *(Interrupting)*: I said I hated . . . I'm sorry. *(Very brief pause)* It'll be better when I go back to work. I can't remember, when did he say?

JENNIFER: He didn't. And I don't think you should rush.

BOB: Well, I have to, sometime. *(Brief pause)* Are we okay?

JENNIFER: What? How?

BOB: I said I was sorry.

JENNIFER: That's not, I don't need you to say you're sorry.

BOB: Okay. Now where are those fireworks?

JENNIFER: I don't think we're finished.

BOB: I'm just wondering if they're going to start up again.

JENNIFER: I just think it's important—

BOB *(Interrupting)*: Seriously, Jen, it's okay. We're great, I promise. Can we just . . . *(Brief pause)* Thank you. I know you're mad, but, thank you.

JENNIFER: Okay. I am mad.

BOB *(Brief pause)*: There's a lot of unsaid things between us. They're there, they're just unsaid.

JENNIFER: Is it good things?

BOB: Yes, it's good things. It's mostly really good things.

JENNIFER: I'm sorry if I get impatient.

BOB: No, it's okay.

JENNIFER: I think I'm pretty patient.

BOB: Then why'd you apologize?

JENNIFER: Because I thought you'd say, "Don't be crazy." I thought you'd say that I was the most patient person in the world.

BOB: So, why not just say that? Instead of dragging me into it.

JENNIFER: Because— God. I didn't drag you into anything.

(Pony enters.)

PONY: Hi. Sorry. You're in the middle of something.

JENNIFER: Yes, we are, actually.

BOB: Hey, Pony. How're you doing?

JENNIFER *(Realizing she won't be leaving)*: Oh, okay. That was quite a show.

PONY: We were celebrating.

BOB: Do you want some wine?

PONY: No, thanks. Is it red? Anyway, no— although that's my favorite. White's good, too. I actually don't care about wine.

BOB: I'm having some.

JENNIFER *(To Bob)*: I'll have a glass with you. *(To Pony)* This isn't the one you brought. We're saving that.

BOB *(Refills Jennifer's glass, but doesn't have any himself)*: There you go.

PONY: We were celebrating finally getting everything out of boxes. Plus, we put that liner paper in all the drawers and cabinets. You should come see it. It's actually not that great. John's asleep so I thought I'd come over.

JENNIFER: Wasn't he just lighting off fireworks a couple minutes ago?

PONY: Yeah, he's weird. No, he's good.

JENNIFER: I wish I could fall asleep like that. Some nights, it's like sleep is—

PONY *(Interrupting)*: The fireworks was so fun and we were playing this music John got at the library, and then he just fell asleep right on the grass.

JENNIFER: I wish I could do that. He's probably still tired from the whole move and the last few weeks.

PONY: Yeah. He saved my life. I could tell you the story, because it's a beautiful story, but just trust me.

BOB: No, I'm sure.

PONY: I'd probably be a real mess. I probably would've overdosed on drugs, if I'd gotten into drugs and then taken too many. *(Brief pause)* People do get saved by people, you know.

BOB: He's really there for you.

PONY: I know.

JENNIFER: I'm sure he'll be fine in the morning.

BOB: How's the house? How's everything else?

PONY: It's mainly that. What I just said.

BOB: What?

PONY: That John had a seizure.

JENNIFER: You said he fell asleep.

PONY: He did, but, like, he was shaking. I don't think it was a seizure. *(To Bob)* Can you go look?

JENNIFER *(Getting up)*: I'll go.

PONY: I gave him his wallet. I know you're supposed to do that. I think he's okay. I was worried I'd hurt him or do something wrong.

JENNIFER: Did you make sure he was— it doesn't matter. *(Exiting)* Where is he?

PONY: Right in the front. *(To Bob)* I'm sorry.

BOB: He's probably tired.

PONY: I thought you'd go.

BOB: No, Jennifer'll figure it out. She should have been a nurse.

PONY: I faint if I see blood. And sometimes even if I don't. I feel like a little kid.

BOB: I'm like that. Everyone's like that.

PONY: No, they're not.

BOB: Well, I'm like that.

PONY: I'm not like you.

BOB: Okay. I'm just saying, don't worry.

PONY: So just say, Don't worry.

BOB: That's exactly what I just—

PONY *(Interrupting)*: I shouldn't be here. I'm scared I'm going to hyperventilate. So I'm taking these little breaths so no one notices me, so that whoever the god is that makes people hyperventilate, he doesn't notice me.

BOB: I'm pretty sure there's not a god for making people hyper—

PONY *(Interrupting)*: That must feel good, being pretty sure of what gods there are and aren't. *(Brief pause)* Sorry. I'm just sort of . . . things are a little crazy at work, right now.

BOB: I thought you worked at home.

PONY: If you can call it work. *(Very brief pause)* I'm sorry if I snapped at you.

BOB: It's okay. Sometimes, over this last year, Jennifer would get so—

PONY *(Interrupting, picking up an unlit candle and smelling it)*: Is this those ones for keeping bugs away? We want to get some of these.

BOB: They work pretty well. The other night—

PONY *(Interrupting)*: I wish I was wearing a sweater.

BOB: Can I grab you a sweatshirt?

PONY: I'm not cold, I just wish I was wearing a sweater. I know what you're thinking.

BOB: You do?

PONY: I married John at the normal age.

BOB: Oh, okay. That's actually not— what's the normal age?

PONY: There's no normal age.

BOB: Well, there must be an average.

PONY: I just mean it seemed like we were young. It's a lot to have to remember, the vows, where you're supposed to stand.

BOB: We wrote our own. I forget what they said, exactly, but they really captured the moment.

PONY: John wanted us to ride off on a horse, but there was some problem with the zoning. He's completely great, by the way. He sort of half disappears, sometimes, probably because I need him to, I guess, because I think sometimes I can only handle half a person, which is probably why I'm attracted to you. I don't mean attracted. Which, God, why can't I, you know, just, I wish I could have more focus.

BOB: That's a lot to respond to.

PONY *(Brief pause)*: So why aren't you saying anything? I should be putting water on his forehead or something. He'll be all right. I'm not a perfect human— sue me.

BOB: No one's going to sue you.

PONY: You don't have to always say something, every time someone says something.

BOB: No, I know.

PONY *(Brief pause)*: John loves listening. He concentrates so hard, it's like he's having migraines. The other night, I was talking about us being old and, he was listening so much, he started crying. *(Very brief pause)* My mother was in the hospital the whole time I was little. That was just, yuck, no thank you.

BOB: I hate hospitals. The smell, the light. You have to leave the car way out in Kingdom Come.

PONY: My aunt got sick from some infection she got from someone in a waiting room. I thought the hospital was, like, some terrible science-fiction thing. The air is gross, too. I know I have it all wrong. I'm done.

BOB: I don't think you have it all wrong.

PONY: I had a number of boyfriends in high school.

BOB: What's "a number"? You had a lot of boyfriends?

PONY: What is this, Ask Personal Questions of the Female Neighbor Night?

BOB: Okay.

PONY: Yeah, exactly. "Okay." That part's over.

BOB: Fine.

PONY: Why are you looking at me like that?

BOB: I'm just sitting here.

PONY: Nobody's ever just sitting here. That's one thing I know.

BOB: Since you don't need anything, I guess I'll go in.

PONY: No, stay. I like your voice. But don't touch me or say anything.

(Lights down, or cross-fade to next scene.)

Scene 7

Night. Pony and John's kitchen. The now-repaired lamp is lit and sitting on the table. John is sitting, a little lost in a haze. Jennifer stands, nearby, or perhaps they have entered together in the transition. Pause.

JOHN: How long have you been standing there?

JENNIFER: We walked in, together, from the front yard.

JOHN: That's right.

JENNIFER: Are you okay?

JOHN: Definitely. I mean, I'm not a doctor or a psychologist, but, I think I'm all right. Although, I'm not a marriage counselor or a beautician, but, yeah, I'm hanging in there.

JENNIFER: You had a seizure?

JOHN: No. Incorrect. You are incorrect, sir. Madam. *(He stares off and slowly straightens his collar or neatens his hair)*

JENNIFER: Why don't we go to the emergency room, just to make sure.

JOHN: I've never seen you at night, except that first time. And another couple times when I was looking over there.

JENNIFER: Pony came over.

JOHN: I asked her to go get you. I didn't want her to see me, if things got ugly.

JENNIFER: What do you mean, ugly?

JOHN: There's a few scenarios. Did you see my stupid fireworks?

JENNIFER: They were sweet. She said you were celebrating.

JOHN: Yeah, I guess that's the word. *(He blinks a few times. Closes his eyes for a second)*

JENNIFER: Is this lamp bothering you?

JOHN: No, come on, I love this lamp.

JENNIFER: I mean the light. You're not seeing, like, little flares in the corner of your eyes, are you?

JOHN: Well, let's see. *(He tries to look into the corners of his eyes. Then stares out, intently. Maybe he imagines himself, very clearly, dying, or, perhaps, sitting in a chair, in a severely disabled state. Brief pause)* Sorry, no. Negative. No little flares.

JENNIFER: Well, that's good.

JOHN: I probably seem like I have it all under control.

JENNIFER: Yeah, you really don't.

JOHN *(Very brief pause)*: I was so glad I couldn't see Pony's face when I went blind.

JENNIFER: I wonder what I looked like.

JOHN: I'm sure you were fine.

JENNIFER: Bob got really claustrophobic. He never believed me when I was saying, one more step this way, or, it's two more steps down.

JOHN: That couldn't have felt very good.

JENNIFER: No. It didn't. Like I would want him to fall down and get hurt.

JOHN: I wish Pony had helped me, but I was glad she didn't.

JENNIFER: You should go see someone and make sure everything's all right. You could go see Bob's doctor, Dr. Leavey. He's a specialist but he's very good.

JOHN: I've seen him a few times.

JENNIFER: You have?

JOHN: That was why we moved here, originally. Don't tell Pony, though.

JENNIFER: You can't just say that.

JOHN: I just did. And please, don't. Come on, you knew all this.

JENNIFER: No, I didn't. How would I know that? What did Dr. Leavey say?

JOHN: What's he supposed to say?

JENNIFER: So, I'm trying to understand, you have HLS?

JOHN: It sounds so sporty when you use the initials.

JENNIFER: God, I'm sorry. This is just, I mean, what are the chances?

JOHN: One-in-something, I guess. Which is really all you need.

JENNIFER: So, you've started treatment?

JOHN: Or, actually, I guess you'd take the total number of people and divide it by the total number of diseases. But I'm not a mathematician. I don't think there's really a treatment, Jennifer.

JENNIFER: Well, we can hope.

JOHN: We can do a lot of things.

JENNIFER: So you're just going through all this alone?

JOHN: Listen, I'm a very spiritual man.

JENNIFER: I'm sure you are.

JOHN: I take it back, actually. I'm not that spiritual.

JENNIFER: Okay. *(Brief pause)* So, when I went into the store the other day, the day I saw you, I was just going in to stare at the international foods. I like the labels. It always calms me down, in a sort of churchy way, I don't know why. And, I figured if I started crying, because I thought I might cry, people would just think I have a dead lover in Barcelona or something. Anyway, you were funny and weird, and you made me feel better. And I remembered people can do that. That talking with someone can make you feel better.

JOHN: What if, after you talk, the other person just stares back at you. With nothing in their heart.

JENNIFER: Are you saying that's what's happening now?

JOHN: No.

JENNIFER: Wait— who am I? I'm the person talking or the one with nothing in their heart?

JOHN: I don't know. I wasn't saying you were either. Can I get you anything? We have instant lemonade. It'll just take a sec.

JENNIFER: No, thanks. I think I understand you, at least a little, and that hurts you somehow. Or it makes you scared.

JOHN: Oh, I'm sure that's true. *(He's found a pack of matches in his pocket. Half to himself)* What is this? "The Aquarium"? Is there a bar around here called The Aquarium? Oh, no—I know where it is.

JENNIFER: Is that some sort of strategy?

JOHN *(Very brief pause)*: I'm sorry, I think I'm just about to leave my body. *(Pause. It's as if he's about to get violently ill, so he's staying still to try to prevent that from happening)* Nope. Well, another time. *(Very brief pause)* Someone threw out this lamp.

JENNIFER: We actually threw out that lamp.

JOHN: Really? Well, you should take it back.

JENNIFER: No, you keep it.

JOHN: Okay.

JENNIFER: It's a nice light. This is nice.

JOHN: I think I might disappear.

JENNIFER: How do you mean?

JOHN: I don't know. Like, physically. Or, mentality. Or, just kind of quietly, on back roads at night. I mean, mentally.

JENNIFER: I'd like to disappear sometimes. No, are you serious?

JOHN: Probably.

JENNIFER: What about Pony?

JOHN: It's all taken care of.

JENNIFER: How?

JOHN: I'm hoping you can check in on her.

JENNIFER: That's how it's all taken care of?

JOHN: I'm not a details person.

JENNIFER: I didn't used to be. That's almost all I am, now. *(Very brief pause)* I'm sure you're a little overwhelmed.

JOHN: I am.

JENNIFER: I like your house.

JOHN: No, you don't. Do you want to do that thing where you think of a number between one and ten?

JENNIFER: Okay.

JOHN: Did you ever have a brother?

JENNIFER: I have two half-sisters.

JOHN: So that sort of equals a brother.

JENNIFER: I had a cousin, my age.

JOHN: I was just wondering. *(He leans his head on her shoulder, or holds her, somehow, clumsily)*

JENNIFER: Is that how you think of me, as a sister?

JOHN: I never had a sister.

JENNIFER: Oh.

JOHN: That's probably what I would've said there, too. "Oh."

JENNIFER: "Oh."

JOHN: Do you know any good lullabies?

JENNIFER: Everything's going to be all right.

JOHN *(Gently moves his head off her shoulder or lets her go)*: No one ever said that to me.

JENNIFER: I just did.

JOHN: Right. But I mean before. When it might've been more true.

(Lights down.)

Scene 8

Darkness. Night sounds. John and Pony's backyard and porch. Bob is caught in a hard cold light that comes on, abruptly. It's a flood-light, activated by a motion detector. Bob stands still. The light goes off. A few seconds pass. The light comes on again: Bob has moved a few feet closer to the sliding glass door. Bob stands still and in a few seconds the light goes off. A few seconds pass. The light comes on again: Bob is looking into one of the glass doors and John is standing at the other.

JOHN: Morning.

BOB: It's the middle of the night.

JOHN: Is that why you're sneaking around my house in the dark, to correct me?

BOB: No. I was just—

JOHN: What? Testing the motion detector on the floodlight?

BOB: No. I was wondering if you were up.

JOHN: Do you make sure we're asleep, too?

BOB: I'm not doing anything wrong.

JOHN: I know. *(Brief pause)* Do you want a drink?

BOB: Maybe . . . if you're having one.

JOHN: We don't have anything. Do you still have that bottle of wine we gave you?

BOB: Yeah, I could go grab that.

JOHN: Nah, forget it.

BOB: No, it's no problem.

JOHN: No, don't worry about it, just drop it off tomorrow. Are you looking for Pony?

BOB: What?

JOHN: Did you just say "what?" to buy yourself a little extra time?

BOB: No. *(Brief pause)* Sounds like you might've been dehydrated, the other night. That's what Jennifer said.

JOHN: Yeah.

BOB: But, you're all right? *(John shrugs)* When Jennifer came over here, did something happen?

JOHN: Something *always* happens. That's the beauty of night. It's the beauty of time itself, John.

BOB: Your name is John.

JOHN: What's your point?

BOB: You just called me John.

JOHN: You knew who I meant.

BOB: So, are you going to tell me?

JOHN: Do you really care?

BOB: I'm standing here, aren't I.

JOHN: That proves nothing. And I'm not even sure how true it is. But, anyway, Jennifer gave me the attention and care that I desperately needed, according to her. It may have gotten intimate, in some sense. There was a sort of humanness, in the air. And, we might have made tacos, I really don't remember. *(The light goes off. They're in total darkness)* Stay still. I know how to handle this . . . *(Brief pause. The light comes on and John is now standing on the other side of Bob)* I was on the other side of you, before.

BOB: I know.

JOHN: That was wild. Okay, I'm going inside.

BOB: No, can you stay? I thought maybe we could talk.

JOHN *(Brief pause as he waits, as if this is something that will be decided by the night sky)*: Yeah, guess not.

BOB: Okay.

JOHN *(Brief pause)*: Good sleeping weather.

BOB: It is. Pony said you sometimes get really sweaty or cold at night.

JOHN: I try to live life to the fullest.

BOB: Just, I get that, sometimes.

JOHN: So?

BOB: I was wondering what you do about it.

JOHN: I sweat, or I start shivering. That usually seems to take care of it.

BOB: Yeah. *(Brief pause)* How's her greeting card thing going?

JOHN: "Her"?

BOB: Pony.

JOHN: I know. Look at the sky. *(Bob joins John in looking up)* No, I'm looking at this part. You look over there.

BOB *(Brief pause)*: It's nice. I like my part I'm looking at.

JOHN *(The light goes off)*: The darkness thickens.

BOB: Yeah.

JOHN: Don't move. *(He makes a quick gesture and the light comes back on)* You moved.

BOB: *You* moved.

JOHN: Let's not fight about who moved. *(Brief pause. Quiet moment of pain. He rubs his temples)* God. Augghh.

BOB: What?

JOHN: Nothing. Ice cream headache.

BOB: Did you just have ice cream?

JOHN: I wish.

BOB: I get those.

JOHN: Wow, we suffer a lot of the same things. High-five. *(He makes no effort to give or receive a high-five)* Ice cream is a dish best served cold.

BOB: Yeah. We switched over to a product made from almond milk. *(Brief pause)* We kind of stopped talking, me and Jennifer. I mean, we talk.

JOHN: People talk about things, or they don't. It doesn't really matter, the things will have their day, the things will rise again. *(He waves or moves, so that the light stays on)*

BOB: I get what you're saying.

JOHN: You don't get what I'm saying. Not your fault. Words don't really do it for me anymore, anyway. It's all just bodies and light. People say it's death and taxes, which, of course, are great, but, no, it's bodies and light. Appearance, disappearance, that's the whole thing. Do you know what a clystophoma is?

BOB: No, what is it?

JOHN: Nothing, it's a totally made-up word. Do you know what an aneurysm is?

BOB: Yeah, of course, that's when your blood vessels—

JOHN *(Interrupting)*: It's another totally made-up word.

BOB: Okay, I get it. A lot of words are made up. *(Very brief pause)* My back is killing me. I used to play football.

JOHN: Try to focus here, okay.

BOB: I am. I wanted to tell you about how I played football. I wanted to focus on that.

JOHN: Were you trying to look into my house?

BOB: No.

JOHN: It's all right. Just wondering. I'm a curious person, by nature. Up to a point, that is, and then I usually completely check out.

BOB: I do that.

JOHN: But I bet you sulk, too. Which is kind of beautiful, sulking. It's very pure, very real. I don't really sulk. I check out. It's been described as breathtaking.

BOB: I think Jennifer thinks I have trouble checking in. *(They both share a little laugh)* Just a couple of guys.

JOHN: A canopy of stars.

BOB *(Very brief pause)*: A couple guys.

JOHN: Be nice to Pony, okay?

BOB: What do you mean?

JOHN: It's the simplest thing I've said all night.

BOB: Yeah, okay.

JOHN: Be nice to Jennifer, too, now that I'm telling you what to do. *(Shakes his head; subtly)* Men. You don't really hear men saying that, you know? Shaking their heads, and saying, "Men." But it's true.

BOB: Men.

JOHN: What position did you play? Do you ever cry?

BOB: It was high school, so everybody played different positions. Fullback. Some defense. I don't really cry.

JOHN: Tell Pony you're old-fashioned. Pretend life is good. She'll like that.

BOB: I think life *is* good. Why are you telling me to do that?

JOHN: I have a plan. Actually, that doesn't really sound like me. *(Brief pause. Quietly)* Fuck.

BOB: What?

JOHN: I just swear, sometimes. And this is giving me a migraine.

BOB: What is?

JOHN: Just, the whole package.

BOB: I should head back.

JOHN: Yeah, get off my stupid rented property. It was great broaching the old questions with you.

BOB: It was. I'll see you, John.

JOHN: Later. *(Turns to head inside)* Oh, hey, Bob? *(Very brief pause)* Pretend I said something really sweet, okay? Like, some gentle, little, good-night sort of thing.

BOB: Okay. *(Brief pause)* Thanks.

JOHN: Sure.

(Bob exits. John goes inside.)

Scene 9

Night. Pony and John's kitchen. Pony is seated at the table. She stands, and absentmindedly picks at the edge of the table or the fringe of the table cloth.

PONY: I never did this. Maybe once. I don't know if I have to look up. Dear God in Heaven, I remember when John and I were coming here, and he started getting a panic attack, and he asked me to say something because there was some noise or voice he was hearing, and he just kept saying, "Please say anything, please say what time it is, or anything," and I didn't, and then he started pulling his hair and hitting the inside of the windshield. We were in a rest area. I don't know why I froze like that. I might've been having my own thing. Which, if I was, please help me with that. He said later it was just a bad patch and it was all right. We even laughed. Please help me be ready, so next time, if John needs me to, I can just say "bookshelf," or "windshield wiper," or sing some campfire song. Because that's not very much to ask. This feels weird. No offense. You probably just think I'm one of so many people. You're probably, like, "My God, what is this even about?" Maybe you're going to burn everything down, anyway. I don't know your crazy mind. You're probably going to burn everything. I just thought I should try. Maybe this was stupid, Lord, but thank you. I hope there's an actual Heaven.

(A brief pause.)

BOB *(Appears at the door)*: Hi.

PONY: Oh, hi. I was actually just, um, yeah . . . I was trying to pray.

BOB: Sorry.

PONY: No, come in. I don't think it'll work.

BOB: I saw the light on. That's our lamp. What were you praying about?

PONY: Different things. I guess, the future.

BOB: I hope it works out.

PONY: I'm not having a crisis. And if I am, I just wanted to try to stamp it out early. *(Very brief pause)* Things are different. I remember how John used to hold me.

BOB: How did he hold you?

PONY: Wouldn't you like to know.

BOB: That's why I asked, yeah. Was it like this? *(He holds her, a little awkwardly)*

PONY *(They stay like that. Very brief pause)*: No. It was different from this. *(They separate)* That was fine, though. That was all right.

BOB: That was just one way.

PONY *(She notices something on her wrist and picks at it)*: This is a little bug bite, I think.

BOB: Sometimes it feels good if you put saliva on it.

PONY: Yeah? *(She gets some saliva on her fingers and puts it on the bug bite)*

BOB: How's that?

PONY: I don't know. It's funny you came by.

BOB: John said I should say hi.

PONY: He did? Where is he?

BOB: He said he was going for a walk.

PONY: Did he have that look?

BOB: What look?

PONY: It's hard to describe.

BOB: He seemed all right. He said I should say hi.

PONY: Hi. *(Very brief pause)* Maybe you can help me with something.

BOB: What? I mean, sure.

PONY: I don't know what you'd call it. *(She presses her hand flat onto his chest)* Self-improvement? But don't get the wrong idea.

BOB: What's the wrong idea?

PONY: Why do you care what the wrong idea is?

BOB: I don't. I just didn't want to be having it.

(Lights fade. They exit together.
John walks uneasily through Jennifer and Bob's darkened backyard.)

Scene 10

Morning. Gray skies. Jennifer and Bob's backyard, porch. Jennifer, seated, with her purse and a sweater. Bob is working on a ship-in-a-bottle, with a screwdriver and a knitting needle. Pony is there, with a backpack.

PONY: This is exciting. I mean, not exciting, exactly— God, I have such a scientific mind. But, it'll be fun.

BOB: It's going to be great. We go to the fair every year. We didn't go last year.

JENNIFER: You said you'd had enough.

BOB: I underestimated.

PONY: I didn't know you did ships-in-bottles.

BOB: I'm actually trying to get it out.

JENNIFER: He thinks it's an antique.

BOB: I said it might be.

PONY: Why don't you just leave it in there?

BOB: Well, you know, it's like, why don't certain people climb Mt. Everest?

JENNIFER: Oh, listen to this, so Bob got us all tickets to the concert at the college tonight.

BOB: I wasn't able to get those.

JENNIFER: You said you did. In those exact words.

BOB: I know. It's disappointing.

PONY: That's all right. What was it, a marching band or something?

JENNIFER: The symphony. We should get going. Where's John?

PONY: He's coming. He went for a walk.

BOB *(Working on the bottle)*: He likes walking, I guess. There's some little thing you turn to collapse the sails. Anyway, I'll put this aside. That looks like a good backpack.

PONY: Yeah, John, um— it's from a store.

JENNIFER: I'm going to get some waters. *(To Bob)* Do you want a water?

PONY: No, thanks.

JENNIFER: I was asking Bob.

BOB: I'm all right. *(Jennifer goes inside)* I was pretending everything was normal.

PONY: Everything is normal.

BOB: Good.

PONY: So, yeah— I don't need to talk about the other night. And the other mornings.

BOB: Good.

PONY: It was one of those momentary things, spread out over a little while. And I felt sorry for you, a little.

BOB: You didn't have to do that.

PONY: No, it felt good. Feeling sorry for you.

BOB: Yeah? I'm glad.

PONY: People don't normally let me in. Or, I don't like going in. It made me feel sort of, I don't know, good. Not like a good person, but, a little bit. Like you're this little kid or weird animal.

BOB: Again, yeah, that's so great.

PONY: I'm trying to branch out. This was one of my branchings out.

BOB: Good.

PONY: I'm trying to face things. I mean, not everything. Oh my God, can you imagine—one person facing everything? But, it feels good.

BOB: It's been a positive, for me, overall.

PONY: Oh, that's so beautiful.

BOB: I could say it with more emotion.

PONY: No, that's fine. I'm important to John.

BOB: I know. I'm just saying, it made me feel better. Like, healthy.

PONY: I'm glad. But this was part of a bigger picture.

BOB: Okay. It was?

PONY: At first, I felt guilty, and then John and I rented a canoe. His shirt was all buttoned wrong and he was chewing a toothpick and I thought we were going to drown. He looked like he had a big secret and I wondered if I did, too. We were laughing and everything was great. It felt right. Just being together and not drowning.

BOB: That sounds great, but, I don't know . . . I'm a living person.

PONY: I know.

BOB: So life goes on, I guess.

PONY: I guess so. I guess so. And that's beautiful. I don't really have an attention span.

BOB: So, this is over?

PONY: I hate when people use the word "this."

BOB: People use that word a lot.

PONY: I did a bad job at a bad thing. I don't feel bad about that.

BOB: I know I get confused. And, I'm confused now.

PONY *(Brief pause)*: I think John wants to take things to the next level.

BOB: You're *married.*

PONY: There's still levels.

JENNIFER *(Enters with bottles of water)*: What's with the hushed tones? You should have one of these.

BOB: Thank you, sweetheart.

JENNIFER: Oh. Well, you are very welcome, sweetheart.

(John, not looking too well, enters from the side of Bob and Jennifer's house.)

Hey, John. We were getting worried.

PONY: No, we weren't.

JOHN: Hey.

PONY: What time does the fair start?

JOHN: It's just fried food and kids running around. It doesn't really "start."

BOB: Yeah, it does. They had a pancake breakfast, this morning.

JENNIFER: It's a lot of fun. I don't really like pancakes, though.

JOHN *(High-pitched and slightly elongated "What?" as in "Are you kidding me?")*: Whhaattt? *(Very brief pause)* No, seriously, what?, I didn't hear you.

JENNIFER: Bob actually just got his hearing tested, the other day.

BOB: Why is that interesting?

JOHN: Did they give you this one? *(He makes a medium-pitch tone, as in a hearing test)* Dooooot.

BOB: They give you a whole range.

JENNIFER *(To John)*: I don't like your tone, mister.

(Jennifer and John share a small laugh.)

PONY: I wish I had something funny to say. My whole thing in my family was being the funny one.

BOB: Say something funny.

PONY *(Stretching her arm, to John)*: I think I slept on top of my arm.

JENNIFER: Are we about ready?

BOB: I'm looking forward to this. This is going to be a lot of fun, Jennifer.

JENNIFER: Are you having a stroke?

BOB: No, I'm fine. In fact, I feel great. I feel like I'm forty-three again.

PONY: I should've brought sunglasses. It's supposed to get sunny. *(She checks her backpack and finds sunglasses)* Oh, good—I did.

JENNIFER *(To Bob)*: Yeah, you should wear a hat.

PONY: Oh, yeah— because, your mother. *(To John)* She had skin cancer. We were comparing about things we're afraid of, the other night.

JOHN: Really? Just kind of sharing fears? We used to do that. Or, we talked about doing that. It was kind of our plan for our— let me finish— marriage.

PONY: It was just a dumb game.

BOB: No, it wasn't.

JENNIFER: Who won?

BOB: It was close.

JENNIFER: I'm sure you did very well. Anyway, ready?

JOHN: You guys go ahead. I'm going to stay here around the— let me finish— house.

PONY: What? No, come on, John, let's go.

JOHN: I don't feel like it.

PONY: You were going to go, a couple minutes ago.

JOHN: Thirty years ago I was going to be a cowboy or a fire engine.

PONY: You were getting ready all morning. I could hear him singing in the shower. It was like a dog howling.

JOHN: I wasn't singing. Singing goes like this *(He speaks normally and does not sing)* Oh, my God, what is happening to me?

JENNIFER: Are you all right?

JOHN *(To Jennifer)*: I'm fine, darling. Sorry, thought you were someone else. I've been drinking.

JENNIFER: You've been drinking?

JOHN: That's what I said, yeah.

BOB: It's ten in the morning.

JOHN: Yeah? What temperature is it? How's the traffic?

PONY: John, don't. Come on.

JOHN: Come on, and what?

PONY: Just come on and go to the fair.

JOHN: I'm sorry, everybody, I don't normally ruin nice weather like this. Especially not at "ten in the morning"— much obliged, Bob. By the way, I wonder, when you and Pony were comparing fears and exchanging fluids, did you happen to use protection? I'm really just asking to ask. A husband gets curious. Although, not that curious, surprisingly. Distance is funny.

PONY: John.

JOHN: Yes? *(Very brief pause)* I said, yes?

PONY: Sweetie, what are you doing?

JOHN: Do I look like I know? *(To Bob)* Who are you?

BOB: What?

JOHN *(Very brief pause)*: No, I know who you are— your name is spelled "Bob." *(He says "Bob" and does not spell it out)*

BOB *(He stands, happening to hold the screwdriver in a relaxed way, by his side)*: Don't be an idiot.

JOHN: That's great advice. And, sorry, just have to check, it's my natural curiosity, again— are you brandishing a screwdriver at me?

JENNIFER: Bob, would you not— don't brandish the screwdriver.

BOB: I'm just standing here.

JOHN: Are you going to gouge my eyes out?

BOB: Do you want me to?

JOHN: Not saying you should, not saying you shouldn't— you just follow your heart.

JENNIFER: Come on, this is ridiculous. Bob, put the screwdriver down.

BOB: I'm not . . . it happened to be in my hand. *(He puts the screwdriver down. To John)* Just stop being an idiot.

JENNIFER: Nobody's being an idiot.

JOHN: *I* am. I thought that's what this was all about.

JENNIFER: Let's just all calm down.

JOHN *(To Jennifer)*: More good advice. You guys know everything! Ooh, I just noticed, I like your hair like that.

JENNIFER: I know why you're acting like this.

JOHN: Yeah?

JENNIFER: You're just confused. I know you're a good person.

JOHN *(Sarcastically)*: Aww, isn't that sweet. *(Brief pause. Sincerely)* That actually is very sweet— thank you. It's really . . . God. *(Moment of frustration and pain in his head, perhaps an almost subliminal sound cue, a low hum or droning sound)* Did anyone else feel that? *(Very brief pause)* The world is about to end. *(He stands, with slight difficulty. Brief pause, as he waits to see if the world ends. It doesn't. The subliminal sound cue fades)* Nope. Wrong again. Sometimes, I don't know why I even try. *(Brief pause)* Pony? Any thoughts?

PONY: Yes.

JOHN *(Vulnerably)*: Oh, sweetie. Don't look at me like that.

PONY: How am I supposed to look at you? I don't know what's going on with you.

JOHN: I . . . yeah. I'm upset.

PONY: I don't know if you are. I've seen you upset. Remember?

JOHN: You're right. Sorry. I'm not being very g-g-gray-graysh. *(Brief pause. He's had a neurological episode. He struggles to remember how a sentence works)* Th-th-the . . . That sounds weird. "The." I'm going to . . . Sorry. *(Begins to exit)*

PONY: John.

JOHN: Hi. *(Exits)*

JENNIFER *(Brief pause. To Pony)*: You should go make sure he's all right.

PONY *(Quietly, gravely)*: Don't . . . I know. *(She exits)*

BOB *(Brief pause)*: I'm sorry, but the whole thing was not what—

JENNIFER *(Interrupting)*: Do not even start. *(Brief pause)* I'm waiting.

BOB: It was kid's stuff. It was getting through the day. I was just kind of managing things.

JENNIFER: No, you weren't. Whatever you were doing. I am so tired of you, I'm so tired of men making speeches and mistakes and being sick and being afraid.

BOB: I know.

JENNIFER: You hurt my feelings. You hurt my feelings every day.

BOB: That's what feelings are for.

JENNIFER: What?

BOB: I don't know.

JENNIFER: No, you don't. That's exactly it. You do not know, Bob.

BOB: I'm sorry. Real life, to me, it's just sitting here, thinking about some dumb thing or when I was a kid.

JENNIFER: That's not real life.

BOB: Well, we're different.

JENNIFER: Yeah? You'd be surprised. Surprise surprise, Bob— something that happens to everyone is happening to you. Get used to it. Be a man. Be a woman, even better. Just stop being a spoiled little angry little teenager.

BOB: You don't have to yell.

JENNIFER: Yes, I fucking do. And I'm not yelling, anyway. I am a person in the world, around you. Do you understand that?

BOB: Yes.

JENNIFER: Do you?

BOB: I'm not a little kid.

JENNIFER: No? How so?

BOB *(Brief pause. Vulnerably)*: I'm tall. I'm taller than little kids are.

JENNIFER: Yes, you are.

BOB: I'm sorry. I'm scared.

JENNIFER: I know. It's scary.

BOB: I don't know what's going to happen. I never know what's happening.

JENNIFER: Well, welcome to— God, I was about to say "the jungle." But, just, I know. It's scary. I think the same things. And I don't know the same things.

BOB: I want to be better.

JENNIFER: We all do. What do you want me to do? Come over and muss up your hair?

BOB: When I was little, I thought I was going to be a good person. Every kid I ever tackled in football, I'd whisper to him, "Are you okay?" when we were getting up.

JENNIFER: Well, that's fine. I'm sure we were all very nice children.

BOB: Every kid. I was in this group that, we used to go sing at hospitals. I liked it and then I couldn't go anymore because I couldn't keep looking at everyone.

JENNIFER: Oh, Bob. You need to drink water.

BOB: No, I don't.

(Lights down.)

Scene 11

Evening. Outside Pony and John's house. John is staring at the sky.

PONY *(Enters)*: Hey. What are you doing out here?

JOHN: I was trying to bend a spoon with my mind.

PONY: Let me see. Where's the spoon?

JOHN: Well, that was the other problem.

PONY: I got you some candy.

JOHN: I love these ones. *(He eats a piece)* Did you get all signed up?

PONY: Yeah. It's getting cooler.

JOHN: It is.

PONY: You know what's weird and scary?

JOHN: I do, but it's always good to hear it again.

PONY: Seriously. To think that you and me aren't the greatest love story in the world. To think that we're just kind of a mess, and we're nice to each other, and we have fun sometimes.

JOHN: Yeah. That's kind of hard to think about.

PONY: I'm sure there's some saying about it. Where, since you can't face that you're not perfect, and not even close, you try to just make yourself into barely nothing. Do we do that?

JOHN: I do.

PONY: I know you hate talking like this.

JOHN: Do you know that thing about how we have all these atoms in us that were there in the Big Bang, when the Universe was formed?

PONY: Yeah. I saw that show with you, remember?

JOHN: Yeah. *(Very brief pause)* That's such a great thing.

PONY: Yeah. *(Brief pause)* Do you have things you're not telling me?

JOHN: No.

PONY: Good. You're sure?

JOHN: No, there is one thing. *(Very brief pause)* I always worried I was going to disappear on you. Just totally leave you in the worst way. It made me feel sick to think it, and I thought it all the time.

PONY: You did?

JOHN: Yeah. I'm sorry.

PONY: Me too. I mean, I thought you might do that. You have that look.

JOHN: Yeah.

PONY: I thought I might too. I always saw myself leaving you. In a really ugly way. Or, just saying bye, and going. Or not saying bye.

JOHN: That's a big relief.

PONY: Come on.

JOHN: No, it is.

PONY: I want to try to solve things with you.

JOHN: Like, crimes and mysteries? I would love that. We can get a van.

PONY: I like how you're always joking around. Sometimes I hate it, though. I just want to solve a few little problems, with you, maybe like five a year.

JOHN: Four.

PONY: Five.

JOHN: Deal. Or, you know.

PONY: Yeah. *(They kiss. Pause)* We don't have any friends or relatives.

JOHN: I know. That's weird. There's those guys. I talked with Jennifer, the other week. They were kind of preoccupied with him, because I guess he had to go to the hospital. I guess he hasn't been doing too well.

PONY: That's too bad.

JOHN *(Very brief pause)*: They want to go out to dinner, sometime. She won a gift certificate.

PONY: That'd be fun. I love gift certificates.

JOHN: Try to enjoy my company during dinner, because I might take off before dessert. Just climb out the bathroom window and vanish into the night, laughing. Or just drop dead, into my salad.

PONY: I wouldn't spend too much time planning, because I might not even show up at all. I'm a totally unreliable person who's filled with terror.

JOHN: Maybe I'd hear that better if you whispered.

PONY *(She whispers)*: Terror. *(They both enjoy it and smile a little)* Now, you do me. "Abandonment."

JOHN: Okay, ready? *(Brief pause)* Actually, can I have a different one?

PONY: Loneliness?

JOHN: Yeah, that's a good one. *(He whispers)* Loneliness. *(Very brief pause. He whispers)* Thank you for the candy. *(Brief pause)* Can I tell you something?

PONY: Do you have to?

JOHN: I guess not. But, I've sort of got this thing.

PONY: So? *(Vulnerably, gravely, a little sadly)* Don't look at me.

JOHN: I like looking at you.

(Lights down.)

Scene 12

Jennifer and Bob's porch. All four Joneses are there, or enter, and sit. John has a doggie bag from a restaurant.

JOHN: That was a good dinner.

PONY: You didn't eat anything.

JENNIFER: I'm glad you could join us.

BOB: Did we use the whole coupon?

JENNIFER: It was a gift certificate.

BOB: I don't care what the word is.

JENNIFER: Okay. *(Brief pause. To Pony)* You all right?

PONY: God, I don't know. I've never seen anyone die. You know, I saw him once, at the post office.

JENNIFER: Poor Elliot.

PONY: It was so much worse than television. All the forks and plates and everything all over the floor. *(To John)* You got white as a sheet.

BOB: Elliot Koford. That was his full name.

JENNIFER: How do you know that?

BOB: We talked.

JENNIFER: I was really surprised, seeing him at the restaurant, just seeing him out, at all. I thought he was at home. I think they were having a special night. Does anyone want a drink? *(To John, who's staring off)* John?

JOHN *(Brief pause)*: Sorry— what? No. I was just thinking.

JENNIFER: About what?

BOB: Thinking. Normal people just sitting and thinking. This is where the magic happens.

JENNIFER: Yeah?

BOB: You know, I'm sorry about— now, wait, who am I talking to, here? *(To John and Pony)* That's right—you two. And, Jennifer. Sorry about all the, just, all the different feelings.

JENNIFER: "Sorry about all the different feelings"?

BOB: Didn't come out right. I just mean it as a blanket apology.

JENNIFER: You know that's not a good thing? A blanket apology? When people say that, it's usually a criticism of the apology.

BOB: Well, there it is, though. It comes from the heart.

JENNIFER *(To Pony and John)*: I gave him two of something he normally only takes one of.

BOB: I supported the idea.

JENNIFER: Just to take the edge off.

BOB: Jennifer felt there was an edge. And I agreed.

JOHN: Apology accepted. In a blanket sort of way.

PONY: "Blankie." Remember? *(Very brief pause)* John was yelling for his blankie in his sleep, the other night.

JENNIFER: You were?

JOHN: How would I know, I was asleep.

BOB: "Blankie."

PONY *(Brief pause)*: So, what was all the blood?

JENNIFER: Oh, I know. The poor man. And he was all dressed up. He looked so proud to be eating at a restaurant. It was probably from an infection in the respiratory tract.

BOB: You know a lot.

PONY: What did he yell? I know, I keep asking questions.

JENNIFER: I think it was something to Hannah. His wife's name is Hannah.

BOB: It was just a lot of yelling.

PONY: It was like when John Wilkes Booth shot Lincoln.

BOB *(Agreeing quickly and completely)*: Yes, it was.

JOHN: Oh, yeah— so, Pony's taking a class.

PONY: Two.

JENNIFER: In what?

PONY: The Civil War and one in Theology.

JENNIFER: Theology, wow.

PONY: I know. It's stupid, but I really like it.

BOB: That's a hard subject. Make sure you study. Moses. Zeus. Am I saying that right? "Zeus." It sounds weird. People took him really seriously, though. "Dear Zeus, please help me with my illness. Please give me a long life on your wonderful planet." You know?

JOHN: Dear Zeus, *(He lifts up the doggie bag—)* please bless this food which— *(—and the bottom of the bag gives way and all the food comes out)* fuck.

JENNIFER: That's all right.

JOHN: The bag got all soggy. I'm sorry.

JENNIFER: It's fine.

BOB: Yeah, just leave it. Someone'll get that.

PONY: But, so, when Booth shot Lincoln, you know, it says in history that he yelled "Sic Semper Tyrannis." It's right there in all the books. But no one who was actually there that night could agree on what he actually yelled.

JOHN: "Auugghh, my ankle."

PONY: He broke his ankle when he jumped onto the stage.

JENNIFER: I just remembered this— wasn't he treated by a doctor named Dr. Mudd?

PONY: Yeah, exactly. Dr. Mudd.

JOHN: It's funny. You do something historical and you scream something important and then you run off and nobody knows what you screamed.

BOB *(Chuckles)*: "Dr. Mudd." I don't think I'd go to a doctor named Dr. Mudd. Ah, maybe I would.

PONY: People were sitting right there, and they couldn't tell you. In real life, it was probably just a bunch of yelling. Like with Elliot. It didn't even sound like words.

BOB: I heard some words in there.

JENNIFER: Yeah. God, that was . . . I felt so happy to see him. And then all that. The poor waiters.

PONY *(Brief pause)*: If they get all the big history stuff wrong, what's anyone ever going to say about any of us?

JENNIFER: Maybe someone'll say something.

JOHN: That'd be nice.

BOB: There's so much crap in the world. Stupid crap and pain. *(Brief pause)* Now where was I going with that? Anyway, I just put it out to the group.

JENNIFER: You're doing really well.

BOB: I have my days. Sometimes, I feel like the luckiest man on the face of the earth. Except for the late Lou Gehrig.

JENNIFER: Sweetie.

BOB: That's a nice word. You said it nice too.

JENNIFER: Thank you. *(To Pony and John)* I'm really glad you guys are over there. That house used to be empty.

PONY: It looked like Elliot was trying to crawl away, like, crawl into the kitchen or something.

BOB *(To John)*: You fix radios, right?

JOHN: No.

BOB: Well then try and fix this one. *(He hands over an old, small portable radio)* It worked the other day.

JENNIFER: I love listening to the radio. You know when you get some little baseball game, a thousand miles away, or the lonely deranged nighttime guy? It just seems like people.

BOB *(To John)*: You can have that, if you want. I haven't heard that owl in a long time.

PONY: Most gods were animals first.

JOHN: I wish there was less words in English.

PONY *(To Jennifer and Bob)*: That's his new thing. How many words there are.

BOB: There's a lot.

JENNIFER: I think it's a good amount.

JOHN: The other night, I was taking out the garbage— see, right there, how many is that? I'm already totally in over my head. But, I was wondering, my life, is it a billion little words, or, is it just one?

PONY: It's just one. Life. Your life.

JOHN: Yeah, maybe. It seems like more. I always think I'm hearing something. But it's like something in my blood. Something's flowing through me. And I was wondering, "What?" Which is scary.

BOB: That is scary. *(Jennifer rubs his arm or shoulder)*

JOHN: So I'm standing there, scared, and leaning on the garbage can and, I thought, maybe it's just me. Maybe I'm flowing through me. And I should just kind of go with it.

JENNIFER: You should. Something is flowing through us. I like that.

JOHN: Me too. And then I got so sick. Remember how sick I got?

PONY: Yeah. It was from an expired yogurt. *(Brief pause)* Oh, do you guys recycle?

BOB: We try to. You can buy different-colored trash cans. *(Very brief pause. To John)* I don't mean to just glide over what you said. I hear you. Go easy, friend. Just do what I do.

JOHN: What do you do?

BOB *(To Jennifer)*: I don't know. What do I do?

JENNIFER: He does a lot. *(To Bob)* You do a lot. I should call Hannah, tomorrow.

BOB: Pony, you're a theologian, let me ask you, do I seem like someone who his middle name is Arthur?

PONY: If it was something else, I'd believe that, too. That's not really theology, though.

BOB: This is great.

JENNIFER: Yeah? What is?

BOB: I don't know— everything. Marriage. The whole life cycle. Whatever John was saying. Just, everything. Boy, I'm really tired. That doesn't affect my point that I'm making, though.

JENNIFER: That everything is great? I think it's a little more complicated than that.

BOB: Aww, Jen. May I call you Jen?

JENNIFER: Sure. Robert.

BOB: You're the best. Life's the best.

JENNIFER: You're in a mood, aren't you.

BOB: Yes, I am. I want to take three of these things, next time.

JOHN *(Brief pause. Little crackles and static from the radio)*: There we go. *(Some different stations, and then an old kind of sad "surf music" song. It plays very quietly)* How's that? It doesn't go very loud.

JENNIFER: That's perfect.

PONY: John can fix anything. *(She moves closer and puts her arm around him)*

JOHN: I just sort of spun the batteries around. I can't fix anything.

(The owl hoots in the distance.)

BOB: I was just thinking about that owl.

JENNIFER: No, you said it. You said it out loud.

BOB: I did? *(He smiles)* I have magical powers.

JOHN: I wonder if Hannah heard whatever he yelled.

JENNIFER: I don't think she did. From the look of her. Poor thing.

PONY: Yeah. *(To John)* Say one of your things.

JOHN: Okay. If you took the night, if you somehow took all the darkness of the night, and then, like, if you have the ocean, or, if you took all the people— *(Brief pause)* Wow, this is a hard one.

PONY: You're tired. You can finish it later. *(Very brief pause. John is shivering)* Are you cold?

JOHN: I'm all right. *(Pony rubs his arm or shoulder)* That feels good.

JENNIFER *(Brief pause. Looking up)*: It's such a beautiful night. The sky is perfect.

JOHN: Yeah. That's my whole contribution. Yeah.

JENNIFER: No, it's good. It's very positive.

JOHN: It's funny—nature. It's just a couple different rules. Laws, I guess.

PONY: I want to be a more outdoorsy person.

BOB: I don't think anything good is going to happen to us. But, you know, what are you going to do. *(Reaches into his pocket)* I forgot, I grabbed some mints at the restaurant. *(He gives one to Jennifer, puts one in his mouth)* I like mints. Mint.

END

Production Notes from the Playwright

In terms of set design, something realistic and detailed but simple enough that we can move quickly from scene to scene, is probably best. In the first production of this play, there was a very large and very high wall, painted black, at the base of which were sliding glass doors, which served as the doors to both couples' houses (i.e., the door out to the patio at one house in one scene, and the door into the kitchen of the other house in another scene). I mention this only because I think the high wall gave some sense of the largeness of the sky and the night and the Universe, and the use of the doors cut down on scene changes. I think transition sounds, such as crickets or buzzing fluorescent lights, are probably better than transition music. Light changes between scenes, as well, should be done in a way that is clarifying and expressive, but also efficient.

In terms of the text, I think all of these characters, though they each have a different mode, have a fairly dry way of speaking. This is not to say that they don't have large and complicated feelings that they're working through. All four characters are trying to deal, in some way, either directly or indirectly or evasively, with illness and death, and therefore with the whole idea of mortality, and therefore with the whole idea of how to live. But they are also just trying to get through the next minute of the day (pick up groceries, etc.). Certain emotional responses, such as anxiety and fear, should probably "leak out" or be glimpsed, rather than being presented in a forceful or muscular way. A straight and simple and serious approach to the play seems best, in terms of allowing for the play's humor and melancholy.

WILL ENO is a Residency Five Fellow at the Signature Theatre in New York, which presented *Title and Deed* in 2012 and *The Open House* in 2014. Following an acclaimed run at Yale Repertory Theatre, his play *The Realistic Joneses* ran on Broadway in 2014, where it won a Drama Desk Award, was named *USA Today*'s "Best Play on Broadway," topped the *Guardian*'s 2014 list of best American plays, and was included in the *New York Times*' "Best Theater of 2014." *The Open House* won the 2014 Obie Award, the Lucille Lortel Award for Outstanding Play and a Drama Desk Award, and was included in both *Time Out New York* and *Time* magazine's Top Ten Plays of the Year. *Title and Deed* was on the *New York Times* and the *New Yorker*'s Top Ten Plays of 2012. His play *Gnit*, an adaptation of Ibsen's *Peer Gynt*, premiered at Actor's Theatre of Louisville in 2013. *Middletown* premiered at the Vineyard Theatre in New York City and subsequently at Steppenwolf Theatre Company in Chicago and at many other theaters and universities throughout the U.S. His internationally heralded play *Thom Pain (based on nothing)* was a finalist for the 2005 Pulitzer Prize and has been translated into more than a dozen languages. His many awards and honors include the PEN/Laura Pels International Foundation for Theater Award, the Horton Foote Prize for Promising New Play, a Helen Merrill Playwriting Fellowship, a Guggenheim Fellowship, a fellowship at the Cullman Center of the New York Public Library, the first-ever Marian Seldes/Garson Kanin Fellowship by the Theater Hall of Fame, and an Edward F. Albee Foundation Fellowship.